Dear Adam

Thank you for your support
and bringing so many smiles to
the ones that matter the most!

Keep # Chasing Greatness
your friend
DME

Thank you so much
for the kind words
I hope this brings
you a smile
Dickie Epps

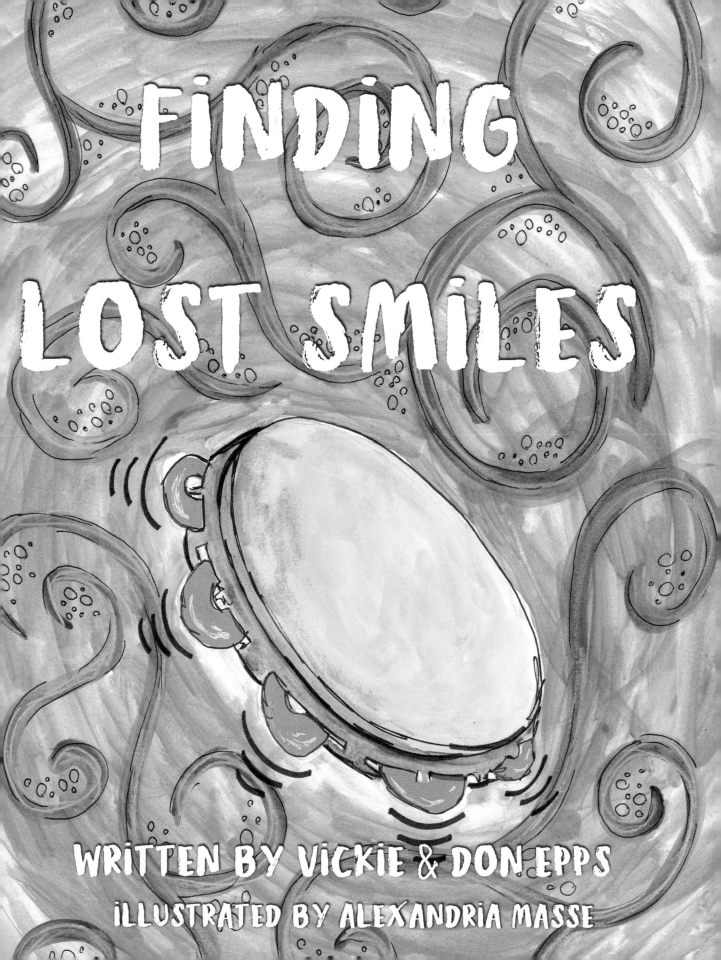

www.codebreakeredu.com

This book is dedicated to our beautiful
children Sarah and Charlie,
who always help us find our SMILE.

Choice time.

Two words. Simple words, but powerful words nonetheless. Two words that perfectly describe what it means to invest in our students. Imagine hundreds of kids engaged in their learning, pursuing their own passions, and fostering their own creativity. Don and Vickie Epps are the epitome of leadership; two very creative individuals who want what's best for kids everywhere and consistently go above and beyond to offer student voice and choice.

I first met Don and Vickie at their home in Chanute, Kansas. We enjoyed a meal, laughter, and a plethora of SMiLES. We talked about chasing greatness, being bold and being humble. I quickly learned how important relationships matter to the Epps family. As I browsed the many family photos hanging proudly on the walls, I understood the passion they have for one another, their own kids and the staff and students they serve.

Finding Lost Smiles is a brilliant story, full of love, energy, and heartwarming illustrations brought to you by two of the kindest people I have ever met. Don and Vickie Epps are the epitome of empathy, kindness, generosity, and leadership. Two people who value rapport above everything else. Two people who always bring a SMiLE to my face. Finding Lost Smiles brilliantly summarizes what it means to be human.

Chasing greatness is helping lost smiles find their home.

Brian Aspinall

EDUCATOR | AUTHOR | SPEAKER

Vickie and Don Epps share an amazing story of kindness and perseverance. This story does a beautiful job showcasing the power one child can have to spread love to others. The message of always trying to lift others up is one that we all need to be intentional at remembering. Share Finding Lost **SMiLES** with everyone in your world!

JANELLE MCLAUGHLIN | EDUCATOR

We all have bad days and lose our **SMiLES**. Vickie and Don Epps have written a story that reminds all of us that simple gestures, like sharing **SMiLES**, can make a big difference and have a positive impact. Every day, I tell my students, "Remember to practice being KIND - Keep It Nice Daily." Now, I'll add Finding Lost Smiles to my story collection to remind my students that you can help others through small acts of kindness. All you need to do is start with a **SMiLE** to help those who have lost theirs.

MARK FRENCH | PRINCIPAL | AUTHOR

A **SMiLE** can go for miles and is contagious - we need to be encouraging others in everything we do-this story certainly does just that!

ANNETTE COZORT | EDUCATOR

The power of a **SMiLE** is immeasurable! Don and Vickie have done an amazing job at showcasing just how much one simple act of kindness can change someone's day. This story is a heartwarming reminder of how we can make our world a better place by spreading kindness, joy and a **SMiLE**.

DAPHNE MCMENEMY | EDUCATOR | SPEAKER | AUTHOR

What a great way to share how, although it's not our responsibility to make someone happy, sharing our happiness and being there regardless of how someone is feeling is a powerful lesson in that we are not alone, and friendship matters. These are two super important tenants in tMHFA and a great precursor for understanding mental health awareness.

KRISTINA MACBURY | PRINCIPAL | AUTHOR | SPEAKER

Finding Lost Smiles is a heart warming story that reminds us all the power of a single **SMiLE**. It is a story of friendship and kindness filled with love. This will be a favorite children's book for years to come!

DARRIN PEPPARD | #ROADTOAWESOME

At different times in our life, we all lose our **SMiLE**. When our children do, it hits home harder than ever. This book shows us that those lost smiles can be found and it's through each other. Beautiful!

LAVONNA ROTH | FOUNDER & CHIEF ILLUMINATOR OF IGNITE YOUR S.H.I.N.E.

You'll **SMiLE**. Plain and simple. This book will put a **SMiLE** on your face, and light up your soul. This is an easy read with a powerful message. A message we all need right now, and always. Read it to your kids, to your students, and to yourself. Read it often. Keep it close by. And when you lose your **SMiLE** this book will be there to help you find it again, just like its authors.

JEFF GARGAS | AUTHOR | COO/CO-FOUNDER, TEACH BETTER TEAM

Can life really be as simple as a **SMILE**? In this charming story, we witness Sam not only sharing his smile but in the end, needing this act of kindness returned back to him. This story is a good resource for teachers and parents in demonstrating how sometimes caring and support for one another can be shared in the simplest of ways.

JENNIFER INBODY | SCHOOL COUNSELOR

Finding Lost Smiles is a heart-warming story of kindness and empathy in a time when we all need it. This book encourages us to be the smile-spreaders and the positivity-pushers. We all know someone who may have lost their smile. Vickie and Don share the perfect story for helping us all find a **SMILE** and brighten the day of those around us!

DR. JACIE MASLYK | ASST. SUPERINTENDENT, AUTHOR

Vickie and Don Epps have crafted a treasure of a story about determination, friendship and the simple act of **SMILING**. Their story is written for all ages to enjoy. We all want our children to be great friends, this book reminds us just how simple it should be. I highly recommend this book for all classrooms, libraries and homes!

ERIC HOOPS | ELEMENTARY PRINCIPAL | FATHER OF TWO
WENDY HOOPS | FORMER TEACHER | FORMER LIBRARIAN | MOTHER OF TWO

Our students live in a world of much hurt and hardship. This book provides us with a critical reminder of how simple, but powerful giving our students hope each day can be by showing them a **SMILE**. All students deserve a smile everyday!

BRITTON HART, ED. D. | DIRECTOR OF LEADERSHIP SERVICES & PARTNERSHIPS
LISA HART | ELEMENTARY EDUCATOR

In Finding Lost Smiles, Vickie and Don Epps tell a simple tale of one of the easiest ways to spread joy to those around us... **SMILE**! The kindness that children show to each other continues multiply. Make everyday a day to find those lost **SMILES**!

JAY BILLY | PRINCIPAL | AUTHOR

Sam is a sweet and lovable child who clearly cares about others. He eagerly shares his **SMILE** with everyone, but he is confused when two new children enter his classroom and don't **SMILE** back. They always seem sad and don't even **SMILE** when it's Chicken Patty Wednesday! He talks to his parents about it and they encourage him to help his new classmates find their **SMILES**. He gets his friends involved in this delightful tale of empathy, kindness and sincere compassion. Sam learns important lessons along the way about what it really means to help someone. Not just children of all ages, but also adults, will not only adore this book, but gain new insight on what it really means to make someone **SMILE**.

JENNIFER LEE QUATTRUCCI | EDUCATOR | MOM | BLOGGER | AUTHOR

The Epps family embodies positivity and gratitude. Their story, Finding Lost Smiles, offers a glimpse into the profound impact they have and insight into the impact we can all have when we are intentional about bringing joy to the lives of others. Don, Vickie, Sarah, and Charlie are experts in inspiring SMILE and #ChasingGreatness.

BRADFORD HUBBARD | ASST. SUPERINTENDENT

Helping one find their SMILE is an investment that costs nothing, but offers incalculable returns. Vickie and Don Epps have captured the truth of helping others find their SMILES while crafting a story that not only engages readers, but helps us find our own SMILE. As we watch our hero, Sam, seek to spread SMILES and find SMILES, we are reminded that there will be times when we are the hero, and other times when we will be the one in need of the hero. A story for young and old alike, Vickie and Don remind us that sharing a SMILE is a guaranteed way to help someone find one. Thanks to the Epps for crafting a story we need to hear, and to Alexandria Masse for illustrating it so beautifully. Read Finding Lost Smiles and release the power of your own!

CHUCK MOSS | PRINCIPAL

Joy is at the intersection of Character, Excellence, and Community. Finding Lost Smiles reminds us that spreading simple acts of kindness is the daily fuel to living a life filled with purpose and meaning. As true Joyful Leaders, Don and Vickie Epps deliver a heartfelt message punctuated by vibrant illustrations aimed at making the world a better place. No doubt readers will walk away with a SMILE of their own!

JENNIFER & HANS APPEL | EDUCATORS | CO-CREATORS OF AWARD WINNING CULTURE

Finding Lost Smiles is a wonderful book with a message of hope and love. The main characters, Sam, Molly and Billy, remind me of so many of our students. Sam never gives up on spreading his message of a joyful SMILE even when it's not returned. Finding Lost Smiles is also an exercise in realizing that what we do is noticed by others even if we don't realize it. Vickie and Don Epps have created a book that will bring a SMILE to your face and can be shared with young and old alike.

JAY POSICK | ELEMENTARY PRINCIPAL

Finding Smiles is beautifully written with a deep and meaningful message about the everlasting power of a SMILE and the importance of friendships. It is an ideal story to reinforce with young students the value and strength of a SMILE. Perhaps most importantly, it demonstrates the potential within us all to positively influence others and support those that may need help finding lost SMILES.

BRIAN MARTIN | EDUCATOR

Sam was a happy kid, a very happy kid.

He smiled all the time.

At everyone in every place.

Sam liked that when he smiled at someone, they always smiled back.

There were two new kids in Sam's class, Molly and Billy.
Molly and Billy didn't smile.
They looked very sad to Sam.
Even when Sam smiled at them, they didn't smile back.

They didn't smile at recess when all the other children laughed and played.

Or at lunch, even when it was Chicken Patty Wednesday!

They didn't even smile when they got to shake the tambourine in music class. Doesn't everyone smile when they shake the tambourine?

That night Sam asked his mom and dad why.

Why didn't Molly and Billy smile at him?

"Well sometimes a person can lose their smile," they said.

"And it can be hard to find it again."

"Lose your smile?" Sam asked, "How do you lose it?"

"Sometimes sad things happen to people and our smile can get lost. But with help, a smile can be found again."

"Do you think I can help them find their smile?" he asked his parents.

"We think you should try," his parents told him.

So Sam decided he had to help Molly and Billy find their smile.

But...How?

How do you help someone find their smile?

Sam decided to do what he always did.

He smiled at them.

Every time he looked at them he gave his best and biggest smile.

But that wasn't working.

He needed more smiles.

So Sam talked to his friends.

"We need to help Molly and Billy find their smiles," he told them.

"How do we do that?" they asked.

"Give them your smiles!" Sam said.

"If everyone is smiling, maybe it will help them find theirs."

So with their plan in place Sam and his friends started smiling at everyone they met.

Soon it seemed like everyone in the school was smiling.

Everyone, but Molly and Billy.

They still seemed sad.

So Sam and his friends worked on their plan.

They decided to do more.

They invited Molly and Billy to play at recess.

And they sat with them at lunch.

And let them shake the tambourine in music class.

Sam and his friends worked really hard at trying to help Molly and Billy find their smiles.

Now we can say we all have bad days.
When we don't get enough sleep,
or not enough to eat.
When the sky turns gray and we
have a cranky day.

So one morning Sam had a bad time.

His favorite hoodie was dirty.

He spilt his cereal on his shoes.

He was grumpy!

His smile was lost that morning.

He stomped into school and scowled down the hall.
And when Sam found his seat in class, everyone stared at him.

His teacher asked, "Sam, is everything OK?"

"Yeah....No....I don't know," Sam answered slouching down in his chair. All of the other kids looked at one another. "What should we do?" they whispered to each other.

Everyone was confused.

Sam made his way to music class later that morning still feeling the grumpy blues.

And as they took turns picking out instruments to play, he felt a tap on his shoulder.

He turned his frowny face around to see who was bothering him.

It was Molly and Billy.

They had a tambourine.

"Playing this always makes me feel better," said Molly as she handed it to him.

"Maybe it will help," said Billy.

Then they both smiled a small but beautiful smile at Sam before hurrying off to pick something out of the instrument box.

Sam looked down at the tambourine and gave it a little shake.
Then Sam looked over at Molly and Billy, and the smile he lost that morning found its way home.

Who are you most like –
Sam, Molly or Billy?
What can you do to
make someone smile?
Have you ever felt like Sam
when he had a bad day?
Do you think Sam's idea of smiling is
a good way to spread smiles?
What other ways can you help
someone else find their smile?
What made Molly and Billy give
their tambourine to Sam?
Sam was spreading smiles even when
he didn't realize it was working.
How do your actions make people
feel even when
they don't say anything?

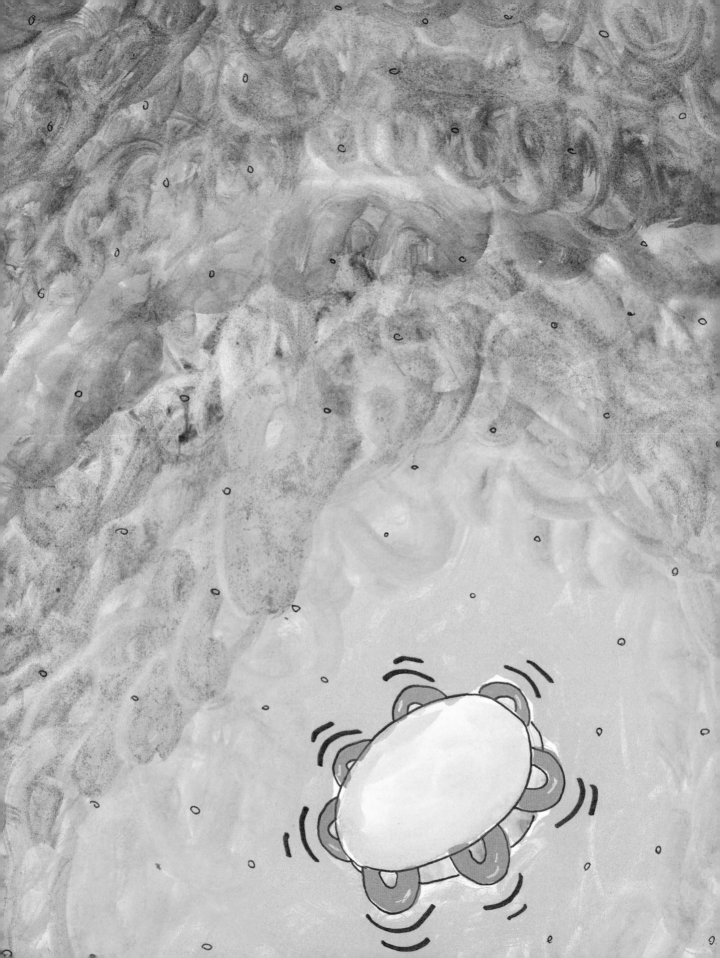

Vickie spent seven years working in the Department for Children and Family Services for the State of Kansas before spending the next six years as a stay at home mom with Sarah and Charlie. Vickie currently serves as a Kindergarten Aide, where she has joy to go to school with her kids everyday. Vickie's experiences have given her a unique perspective on life that she captures in story. Vickie enjoys teaching her kids how to cook but absolutely hates folding laundry.

An educator for the last 19 years, Don Epps, has served as a classroom teacher, coach, high school principal and currently a middle school principal. The #ChasingGreatness Principal has been featured in national publications for stories of school culture transformation in creating what is now known as "Frosty Moments". Epps also is known in the education world for his uplifting videos posted on social media that feature his own unique blend of motivation, comedy and inspirational content that promotes positivity. Most importantly Don is the proud husband to Vickie and the father to Sarah and Charlie, the most important team in his life.

CONNECT WITH VICKIE & DON EPPS

 @VickieEppsEDu

 @DonEppsEDU

 eppsEDU@gmail.com

Vickie and Don have woven together a beautiful story that will touch your heart and inspire you to help others find their lost **SMiLE**! This is the perfect book for every classroom and every home.

ALICIA RAY | MOTHER | EDUCATOR | AUTHOR

SMiLES are infectious and can change someone's time, day, and even life. In this book, Sam shows us all that we might not always have the best days, but those days and our attitudes can change when we find our lost **SMiLES**.

RYAN SHEEHY | PRINCIPAL | AUTHOR

Don and Vickie Epps have created a masterpiece that all educators need to have on display in their classrooms, as well as parents in their home libraries. Finding Lost Smiles isn't a story just for our kids and students. This story is a reminder to all of us that we can never give up on trying to be the light for others. It may seem like we are not making progress reaching those that have lost their **SMiLES** and bringing them into the light. There will come a day, if we are persistent and determined to be there for others no matter what, where we will see our hard work shine through the cracks. I look forward to not only sharing Finding Lost Smiles with my students and staff, but my own children as well to teach them to be the guide for helping others find their lost **SMiLES**.

MICHAEL EARNSHAW | PRINCIPAL | AUTHOR

Finding Lost Smiles is an inspiring book about the power of everyone's individual **SMiLES**! Vickie and Don provide a relevant, positive look into the social emotional experiences that students face each day. This is a perfect book for elementary aged students and is guaranteed to leave you with your **SMiLE** on for all to see.

DR. ERIC CARLIN | ELEMENTARY PRINCIPAL

This short, yet powerful story illustrates real-life examples of what many of the children in our society go through each day – something or someone in their young life has robbed them of their **SMiLE**. Further, it highlights the influence that just one person can have upon impacting their school and the environment for other students. Finding Lost Smiles is a real-life anecdotal reminder of the power that each of us has to help lift those around us. I would strongly encourage educational leaders, teachers, and students alike to spend some time in the message that this book has to offer – our school buildings will be better places of love and understanding as a result of applying the principles found in this book.

DR. KELLEN ADAMS | SUPERINTENDENT | PROFESSOR

Finding Lost Smiles captures the essence of what the real-world classroom environment is like. This book is an excellent reminder for students to take notice of their surroundings, and specifically other students around them that may be struggling with everyday life. This story serves as an example of having compassion and understanding for our peers, as well as actively seeking to help make their life better. We should all be more like Sam everyday – aware of the lost **SMiLE** that are walking around us and prepared to help share ours with others.

CORINNA ADAMS | EDUCATOR

Don and Vickie Epps' inspiring book Finding Lost Smiles contains an uplifting message and whimsical illustrations by Alexandria Masse. The story serves as a fundamental model for young people about how they should treat others and how they can take care of their friends and loved ones when life doesn't go perfectly. The best part, of course, is that by the end of the book, I was the one who was **SMILING**. I suspect you will be, too. And what's better than that?

DAN TRICARICO | AUTHOR

My heart was touched as I read Finding Lost Smiles. The story of lost **SMILES** can be found on every one of our schools each day. We don't have to always know the reason why, but we can have a powerful impact by showing kindness and recruiting others to do the same. The outcome will be, Finding Lost Smiles.

JIM SPORLEDER | TRAUMA INFORMED CONSULTANT | SPEAKER

I really liked this book. Sometimes I lose my **SMILE** and am sad. I really liked learning how other kids can help me and I can help them.

CAYDEN SCHMITTOU | STUDENT

This book is amazing. As an adult I can testify that Don has helped me find my own **SMILE** more times than I can count. The fact that he is using his infectious gift to help children as well as adults makes me **SMILE** even more than normal. Thank you, Don and Vickie for sharing your gift with us.

DAVE SCHMITTOU | CAYDEN'S DAD | AUTHOR | EDUCATOR

Reading Finding Lost Smiles is like seeing a rainbow after a storm or hearing a baby laugh...you can't help but **SMILE** . It's a simple, but powerful story about sharing one of the most important possessions we have as humans, our **SMILE**. It's a great way to show our students and our own children the impact we can make on others, even when we don't realize it. I recommend this book to anyone looking to spread a little sunshine and for those who may need a reminder of the magic a **SMILE** can bring.

JONATHON WENNSTROM | ELEMENTARY SCHOOL PRINCIPAL

Finding Lost **SMILES** is a beautifully written story about the power of kindness and one's ability to make a difference in someone's life. This story is a must read, as children need to continue to be surrounded by positive messages that lift them up and promote empathy, acceptance, and love!

JONATHAN ALSHEIMER | EDUCATOR | AUTHOR | KEYNOTE SPEAKER

Who doesn't love Chicken Patty Wednesday?! Finding Lost Smilies is a perfect nighttime read with the family or mentor text to model moods for students. Follow Sam, Molly, and Billy as they deal with truly difficult situations and share an important message with readers. Go find your **SMILE**!

RAE HUGHART | TEACHBETTERTEAM

Don't miss these titles

RISK TAKER
Strengthen Your Courage, Blaze A New Trail and Ignite Your Students' Passions

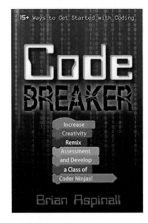

Code BREAKER
Increase Creativity, Remix Assessment, and Develop a Class of Coder Ninjas

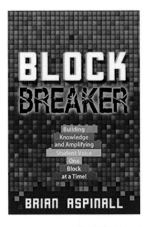

BLOCK BREAKER
Building Knowledge and Amplifying Student Voice One Block at a Time

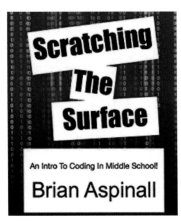

Scratching The Surface
An Intro to Coding in Middle School

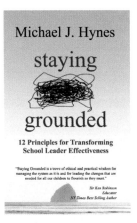

Staying Grounded
12 Principles for Transforming School Leader Effectiveness

ROCK YOUR CLASS
Creatively impactful teacher rockstar tips from A to Z

HALLWAY CONNECTIONS
Autism and Coding

THINK LIKE A CODER
Connecting Computational Thinking to Everyday Activities

Gracie
**An Innovator Doesn't Complain About The Problem.
She Solves It!**

www.codebreakeredu.com

Made in the USA
Coppell, TX
14 May 2020